English to a Beat!

Jane Zion Brauer

Practice Book

HAMPTON-BROWN

Contents

Skills Practice

Writing Projects

Skill Tests

Statements with *I am*

👓 Look at the picture.

✏️ Choose a word or words from the box to complete each sentence.
Write the word or words.

> I   am   I'm

1. I ___*am*___ Boris.

2. _____ am 13 years old.

3. I _____ from Russia.

4. _____ a good artist.

5. _____ happy.

6. _____ funny.

I am Boris.

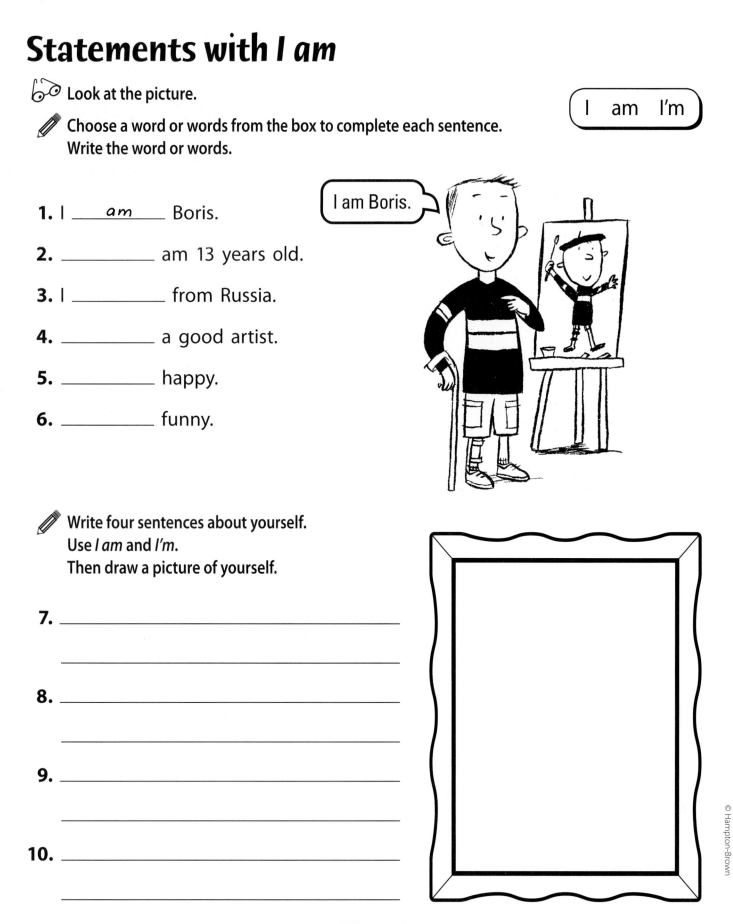

✏️ Write four sentences about yourself.
Use *I am* and *I'm*.
Then draw a picture of yourself.

7. _____

_____

8. _____

_____

9. _____

_____

10. _____

_____

Statements with *You are*

👓 Read the sentences.

✏️ Choose a word from the box to complete each sentence.
Write the word.

> You   are   You're

1. I am big. You ___are___ little.

2. _____ are so pretty.

3. _____ are a good tailor.

4. _____ a fast worker!

5. Now you _____ big!

6. _____ little again.

Statements with *Is* and *Are*

👓 Read the sentences. Look at the picture.

✏️ Write *is* or *are* to complete each sentence.

1. The dress _____is_____ not right.

2. The dress _____ too big.

3. The gloves _____ not right.

4. The gloves _____ too small.

5. The shoes _____ too big.

6. The shoes _____ too loose.

7. The hat _____ the right size.

8. The hat _____ perfect!

✏️ Write a sentence about each picture. Use *is* or *are*.

9. *The socks* _____

10. *The jacket* _____

11. *The boots* _____

12. *The skirt* _____

Pronouns: *I, You, We*

👓 Look at the pictures.

✏️ Write *I*, *You*, or *We* to complete each sentence.

Pronouns: *He, She*

 Look at the pictures. Read the sentences.

 Change the underlined word to a pronoun. Write *He* or *She*.

 1. <u>Mom</u> digs in the garden.

_____*She*_____ digs in the garden.

 2. <u>Grandma</u> has a big hat.

_____ has a big hat.

3. <u>Dad</u> picks the peppers.

_____ picks the peppers.

4. <u>Ahn</u> sprays the water.

_____ sprays the water.

5. <u>Tran</u> runs away!

_____ runs away!

 6. <u>Dad</u> smiles.

_____ smiles.

© Hampton-Brown

Pronouns: *It, They*

Look at each picture. Read the sentences.

Change the underlined words to a pronoun.
Write *It* or *They*.

1. <u>Boris and Lena</u> get carrots.

_____They_____ get carrots.

2. <u>The carrots</u> are big.

_____ are big.

3. <u>The carrot</u> is good.

_____ is good.

4. <u>Nura and Hadi</u> get tomatoes.

_____ get tomatoes.

5. <u>The tomatoes</u> are beautiful.

_____ are beautiful.

6. <u>The bag</u> is full!

_____ is full!

Name _____ Date _____

Questions with *Can*

 Look at the picture.

✏️ Choose words from the box to complete each question and answer. Write the words.

| Can can can't |
| Yes   No |

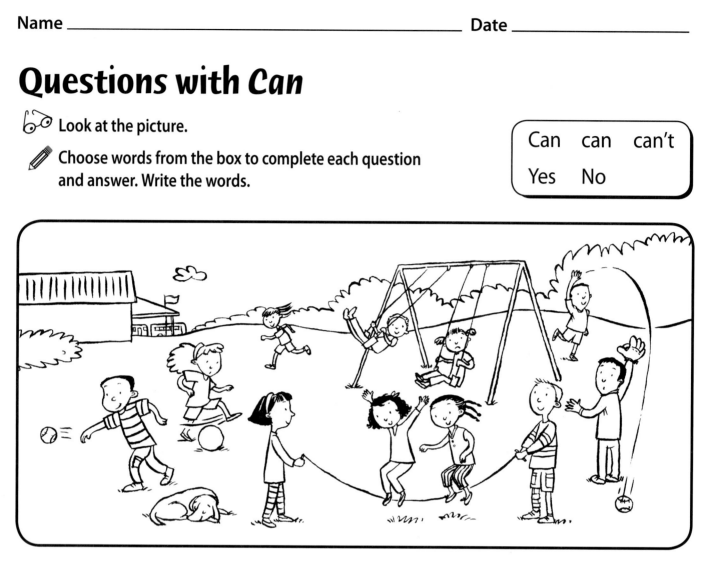

Questions

1. ___Can___ the boy catch the ball?

2. _____ the girl kick the ball?

3. _____ the boy throw the ball?

4. _____ the girl run?

5. _____ the kids jump?

6. _____ the dog play?

7. _____ the boy swing up high?

8. _____ the girl swing up high?

Answers

No, he ___can't___.

_____, she can't.

Yes, he _____.

_____, she can.

Yes, they _____.

No, he _____.

Yes, he _____.

No, she _____.

Questions with *Is* and *Are*

📖 Look at pages 20–21 in *Can Turtle Fly*?

✏️ Choose words from the box to complete each question and answer. Write the words.

Is	is	isn't
Are	are	aren't

Questions

1. ___*Are*___ the birds in the sky?

2. _____ Turtle in the sky?

3. _____ Turtle sad?

4. _____ the clouds dark and gray?

5. _____ the stick in Turtle's mouth?

6. _____ the trees and mountains small?

7. _____ Turtle happy?

8. _____ the trees in the sky?

Answers

Yes, they ___*are*___.

Yes, he _____.

No, he _____.

No, they _____.

Yes, it _____.

Yes, they _____.

Yes, he _____.

No, they _____.

📖 Now look at pages 22–23 in *Can Turtle Fly*?

✏️ Write questions about the picture.

🧍🧍 Find a partner. Ask your questions.

9. *Is* _____

10. *Is* _____

11. *Are* _____

12. *Are* _____

Who? What? When? Where?

👓 Look at each picture. Read the question.

✏️ Write the answer.

In the Question	In the Answer
Who	a person
What	a thing
When	a time
Where	a place

1.

Where is the kite?

The kite is in the air.

2.

When is lunch?

_____

3.

Who is on the swing?

_____

4.

What is in the basket?

_____

✏️ Write four more questions.

👫 Have a partner answer the questions.

5. *Who* _____

6. *What* _____

7. *When* _____

8. *Where* _____

Commands

👓 Look at the map. Follow the numbers.

✏️ Write a command for each number. Tell Janell what to do.

Commands
Walk to the _____ .
Go to the _____ .
Stay on the _____ .
Leave the _____ .

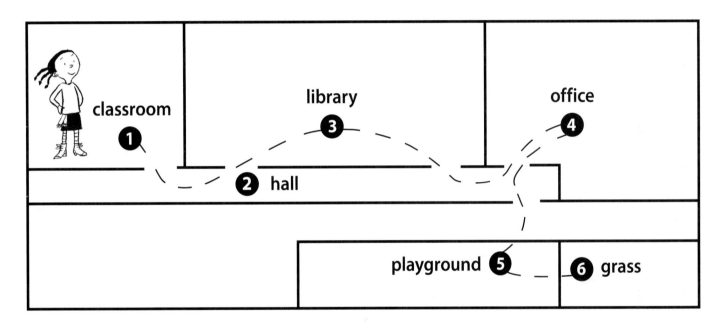

1. *Leave the classroom.* _____

2. _____

3. _____

4. _____

5. _____

6. _____

Questions and Exclamations

👓 Read each sentence.

✏️ Write a question mark (?) or an exclamation point (!).

1. Is the fire gone ?_____

2. The fire is gone _____

3. Is the elephant happy _____

4. The elephant is angry _____

5. Are the bees in the elephant's nose _____

6. Will the bees leave _____

7. The elephant blows and blows _____

8. Can the bees find a new home _____

9. Where will the bees go _____

10. The elephant's nose is very long _____

👓 Look at pages 28–29 in *Leave, Bees!*

✏️ Write two questions and two exclamations about the pictures.

11. **Question:** _____

12. **Question:** _____

13. **Exclamation:** _____

14. **Exclamation:** _____

Statements with Not

👓 Look at the picture. Read each question.

✏️ Write the answer. Use *not*.

1. Is the door open? *No, the door is not open.* _____

2. Is the police officer inside? _____

3. Are the boys in the car? _____

4. Are the boys scared? _____

5. Is the librarian angry? _____

6. Is the police officer worried? _____

7. Are the boys at home? _____

8. Is the librarian in the car? _____

9. Are the boys on the steps? _____

10. Is it a rainy day? _____

Action Verbs with -ing

👓 Look at each picture.

✏️ Choose a word from the box to complete each sentence.
Add -ing. Write the new word.

walk	eat	talk
play	smell	sing

1.

They are ___eating___ breakfast.

2.

She is _____ to school.

3.

She is _____ a song.

4.

She is _____ the soup.

5.

They are _____ to Dad.

6.

They are _____ a game.

Action Verbs with -*ing*

👓 Look at the picture.

✏️ Use each group of words to write a question. Add a question mark.

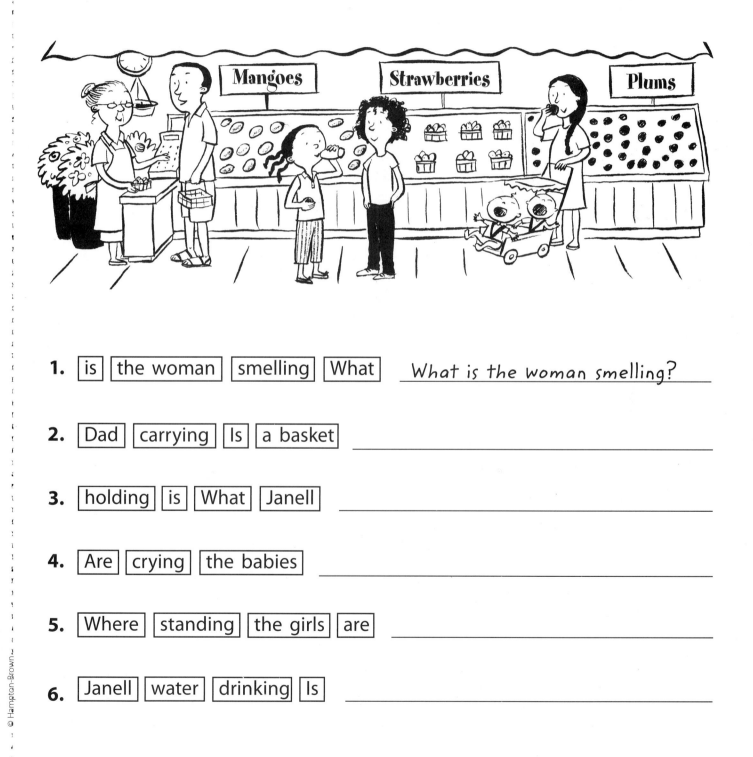

1. │is│ │the woman│ │smelling│ │What│   *What is the woman smelling?*

2. │Dad│ │carrying│ │Is│ │a basket│ _____

3. │holding│ │is│ │What│ │Janell│ _____

4. │Are│ │crying│ │the babies│ _____

5. │Where│ │standing│ │the girls│ │are│ _____

6. │Janell│ │water│ │drinking│ │Is│ _____

Action Verbs with -ing

 Look at each picture. Read the question. ✏ Write the rest of the answer.

1. Are you eating a mango? No, I _am not eating a mango._

2. Are you eating a plum? Yes, I _____

3. Is the cat drinking milk? No, it _____

4. Are the cats drinking water? Yes, they _____

Name _____ Date _____

Nouns

👓 Look at each picture.

✏️ Write a word from the box to name the picture.
Tell if it is a **person**, **animal**, **place**, or **thing**.

cook	town	farm
horse	king	pot
tree	chick	

1. chick
animal

2. _____

3. _____

4. _____

5. _____

6. _____

7. _____

8. _____

©Hampton-Brown

Plural Nouns with -s

👓 Look at the picture. Read each sentence.

✏️ Change the word below the blank to tell about more than one. Write the new word.

1. The little ___chicks___ are in the barnyard.
          chick

2. There are two _____ in the barnyard, too.
                 pig

3. The _____ sit on the fence. They watch the pigs.
          girl

4. The _____ have a lot of apples on them.
          tree

5. The hungry _____ eat the sweet apples.
            horse

6. The _____ are hungry, too! They run to the barn.
          goat

7. There are two _____ standing in the barn.
             farmer

8. The _____ fly over the barn.
          bird

Irregular Plural Nouns

 Look at the picture. Read each sentence.

✏ Change each sentence to tell about more than one.
Use a word from the box. Write the new sentence.

children	mice
women	feet
geese	men

1. The child is swimming.

_The children are swimming._____

2. The goose is flying.

_____

3. The woman is eating.

_____

4. Her foot is in the water.

_____

5. The mouse is running.

_____

6. The man is working.

_____

Name _____   Date _____

Adjectives That Tell How Many

1 one	6 six
2 two	7 seven
3 three	8 eight
4 four	9 nine
5 five	10 ten

Look at the pictures. Read what Simon says.

Write number words to tell how many more of each item Simon needs.

Ten people are coming to my party!

1. Simon has **three** . He needs _seven_ forks.

2. Simon has **six** . He needs _____ plates.

3. Simon has **two** . He needs _____ chairs.

4. Simon has **seven** . He needs _____ cups.

5. Simon has **five** . He needs _____ spoons.

6. Simon has **eight** . He needs _____ napkins.

Look at the pictures.

Write two sentences about the things for Simon's party. Use number words.

7. _____

8. _____

Adjectives That Describe

blue	red	long
brown	big	round
green	little	square

✏️ Color the picture.

✏️ Complete each sentence. Use two different words from the box. Write the words.

1.

It's a _brown_ box.

The box is _square_ .

2.

It's a _____ bag.

The bag is _____ .

3.

It's a _____ scarf.

The scarf is _____ .

4.

It's a _____ car.

The car is _____ .

5.

It's a _____ ball.

The ball is _____ .

6.

It's a _____ hat.

The hat is _____ .

This, That, These, Those

this	these
that	those

👓 Read each person's sentence. Find the food in the picture.

✏️ Write a word from the box to complete the sentence.

1. ___This___ soup smells good!

2. _____ cake over there is pretty.

3. Please pass _____ cookies to me.

4. _____ noodles are really hot!

5. Would you like _____ green beans?

6. _____ ham looks so yummy!

7. Will you pass _____ potatoes to me?

8. May I have _____ salt, please?

Subjects and Action Verbs

run	climb
sit	jump
race	drink

👓 Look at the pictures.

✏️ Choose a word from the box to complete each sentence. Write the word.

1. You __run__ fast!

2. We _____ against each other. We _____ high.

3. I _____ on the grass. I _____ some water.

4. They _____ the wall.

✏️ Write two more sentences. Use action verbs. Start your sentences with *I, You, We,* or *They.*

5. _____

6. _____

Action Verbs with -s

👓 Read the sentences.

✏️ Choose the correct verb. Write it in the blank.

1. I _____*throw*_____ the ball into the air.
   throw / throws

2. Janell _____ toward the ball.
   run / runs

3. Janell is too slow! The ball _____ to the ground.
   fall / falls

4. The people watch. They _____ loudly.
   yell / yells

5. José _____ the ball. It _____ from his hands!
   grab / grabs   slip / slips

6. Janell _____ the ball. She _____ to the line.
   get / gets   race / races

7. We _____ the game! The people _____ .
   win / wins   cheer / cheers

✏️ Write three more sentences about a game. Use action verbs.

8. *She* _____

9. *He* _____

10. *It* _____

Verbs: *Have* and *Has*

✏️ Complete each sentence. Write *have* or *has*.

1. The Sky God ___*has*___ a gift for Anansi.

2. Now Anansi _____ all the wisdom in the world!

3. He climbs a tree. It _____ a tall trunk.

4. The animals _____ a question. They ask why Anansi falls.

5. Anansi's son _____ an idea.

6. Anansi's son _____ more wisdom than Anansi.

7. Anansi breaks the pot! Now, I _____ wisdom.

8. You _____ wisdom, too!

✏️ Write two more sentences about Anansi or another character.
Use *have* or *has*.

🏃🏃 Read your sentences to a partner.

9. _____

10. _____

Name _____ Date _____

Nouns with 's

👓 Look at the pictures.

✏️ Write the correct noun to complete each sentence. Add 's.

cook

judge

María

farmer

baker

1. This is the ___cook's___ spoon.

2. This is the _____ basket.

3. This is the _____ cup.

4. These are the _____ rolls.

5. This is _____ brush.

6. This is the _____ bowl.

7. This is the _____ hat.

8. This is the _____ tray.

Pronouns: My, Your, Our

Look at the pictures.

Choose the correct pronoun to complete each sentence. Write the word.

1. Welcome to The Clothes Line! This is ____my____ store.

my / I

2. You have nice clothes in _____ store.

your / my

3. This is _____ favorite place to shop.

our / we

4. We always buy _____ clothes here.

I / our

5. This is not my hat. Is it _____ hat?

your / you

6. Yes, it is _____ hat. Thank you!

our / my

© Hampton-Brown

Pronouns: *His, Her, Its, Their*

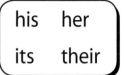

👓 Look at pages 20–27 in *María and the Baker's Bread*.

✏️ Complete each sentence. Write a pronoun from the box.
Be sure it goes with the underlined part of the sentence.

his	her
its	their

1. At the court, <u>the baker</u> tells _____*his*_____ story.

2. Then, <u>María</u> tells _____ story.

3. María talks about <u>the bread</u>. She loves _____ smell.

4. <u>The judge</u> will think about _____ answer.

5. <u>The courthouse</u> closes. People wait outside _____ doors.

6. Finally, <u>the judge</u> gives _____ answer to María and the baker.

7. <u>He</u> wants María to put three coins in _____ cup.

8. <u>The friends</u> help María. They put _____ coins in the cup.

9. The judge shakes <u>the coins</u>. Everyone hears _____ sound.

10. The judge tells <u>María</u> to keep _____ coins.

11. <u>She</u> celebrates with _____ friends.

12. The baker is mad! <u>He</u> shakes _____ fists.

Name _____ Date _____

Verb Tense

👓 Look at the picture. Read each sentence.

✏️ Change the verb to tell about the past. Write the new sentence.

1. The ants <u>crawl</u> over the log.

   The ants crawled over the log.

2. The frog <u>kicks</u> his legs.

   _____

3. The spider <u>walks</u> on the leaf.

   _____

4. The leaf <u>covers</u> some sticks.

   _____

5. The grasshopper <u>jumps</u> over the rocks.

   _____

6. The birds <u>land</u> on the grass.

   _____

Name _____ Date _____

Actions in the Past: -ed

 Look at the picture.

✏️ Change the word in front of each sentence to tell about the past.
Write the new word.

show   **1.** Simon _showed_ his mouse to the class.

smile   **2.** Janell _____ at the nice mouse.

like   **3.** Janell _____ its cute little nose.

close   **4.** Nura _____ her eyes.

hate   **5.** She _____ the scary mouse!

walk   **6.** José _____ to the cage.

play   **7.** He _____ with the mouse.

touch   **8.** His hand _____ the soft fur.

smell   **9.** The mouse _____ his fingers.

decide   **10.** José _____ to get a mouse, too!

Actions in the Past: -ed

👓 Look at each picture.

✏️ Change the word under the blank to tell about the past. Write the word.

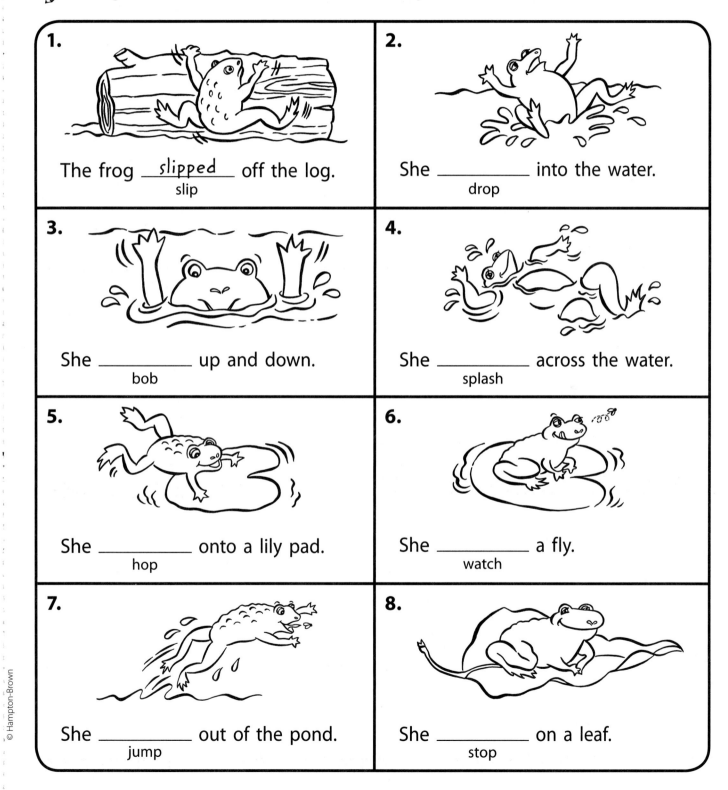

1. The frog __slipped__ off the log.
slip

2. She _____ into the water.
drop

3. She _____ up and down.
bob

4. She _____ across the water.
splash

5. She _____ onto a lily pad.
hop

6. She _____ a fly.
watch

7. She _____ out of the pond.
jump

8. She _____ on a leaf.
stop

Location Words: *In, On*

👓 Look at pages 12–13 in *Juan Bobo Goes Up and Down the Hill*.

✏️ Write *in* or *on* to complete each sentence.

1. Grandma is _____*in*_____ the house.

2. The hat is _____ Juan's hand.

3. The cupboard is _____ the floor.

4. The shelf is _____ the cupboard.

5. The dishes are _____ the shelf.

6. The black pot is _____ the cupboard.

7. The bowl is _____ the shelf.

8. The coconuts are _____ the bowl.

👓 Now look at page 14 in *Juan Bobo Goes Up and Down the Hill*.

✏️ Write three sentences about the picture. Use *in* and *on*.

9. _____

10. _____

11. _____

👓 Read the sentences.

✏️ Draw a picture about them in the box.

12. The table is in the kitchen. The bowl is on the table. Some fruit is in the bowl.

More Location Words

👓 Look at the pictures.

✏️ Choose a word or words from the box to complete each sentence. Write the word.

below	inside	in front of
behind	above	beside
next to	under	

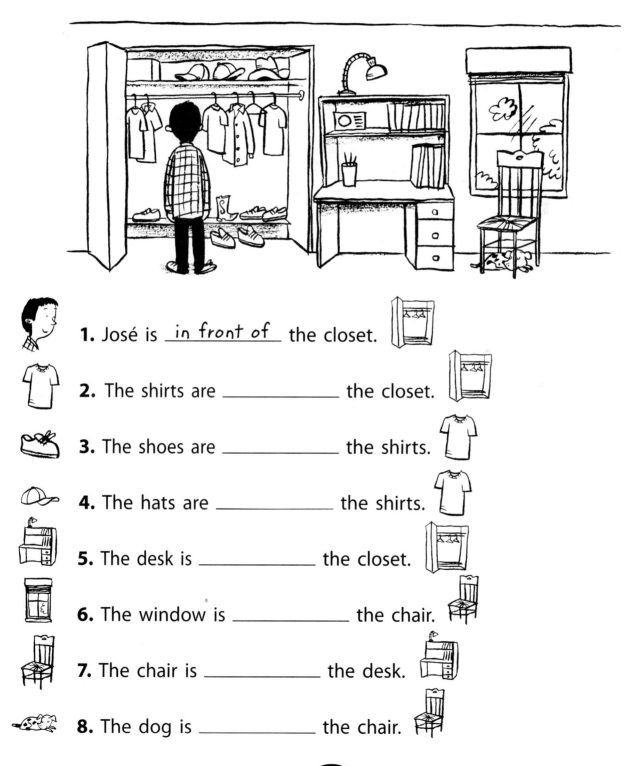

1. José is ___in front of___ the closet.

2. The shirts are _____ the closet.

3. The shoes are _____ the shirts.

4. The hats are _____ the shirts.

5. The desk is _____ the closet.

6. The window is _____ the chair.

7. The chair is _____ the desk.

8. The dog is _____ the chair.

Name _____ Date _____

Direction Words

👓 Look at the picture. Follow the arrows.

✏️ Choose a word from the box to complete each sentence.
Write the word.

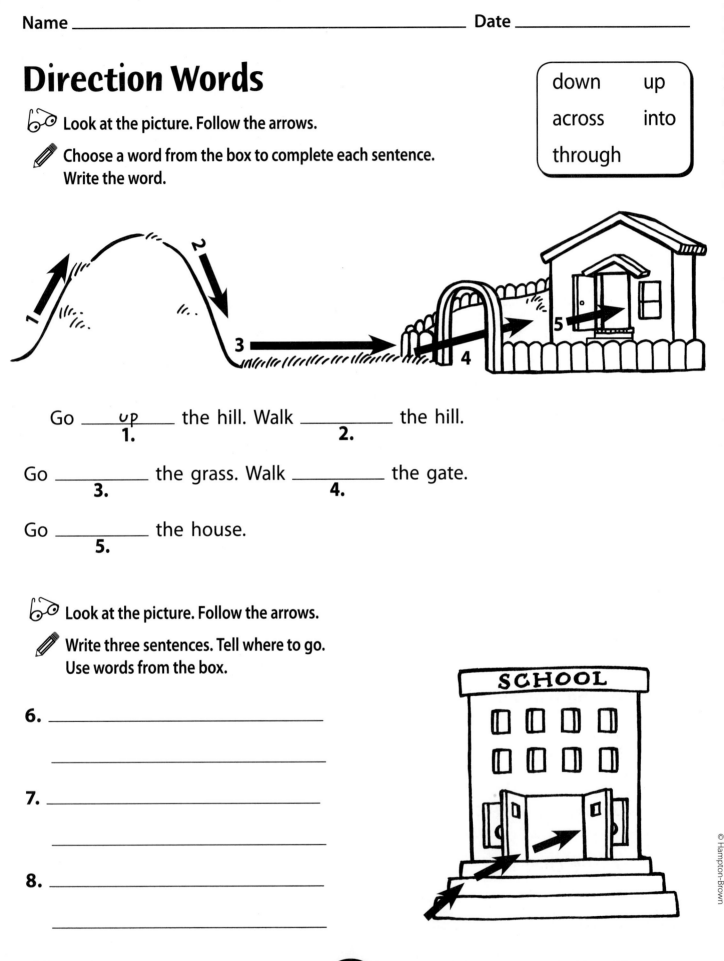

down	up
across	into
through	

Go ____up____ the hill. Walk _____ the hill.
     1.   **2.**

Go _____ the grass. Walk _____ the gate.
   3.   **4.**

Go _____ the house.
   5.

👓 Look at the picture. Follow the arrows.

✏️ Write three sentences. Tell where to go.
Use words from the box.

6. _____

_____

7. _____

_____

8. _____

_____

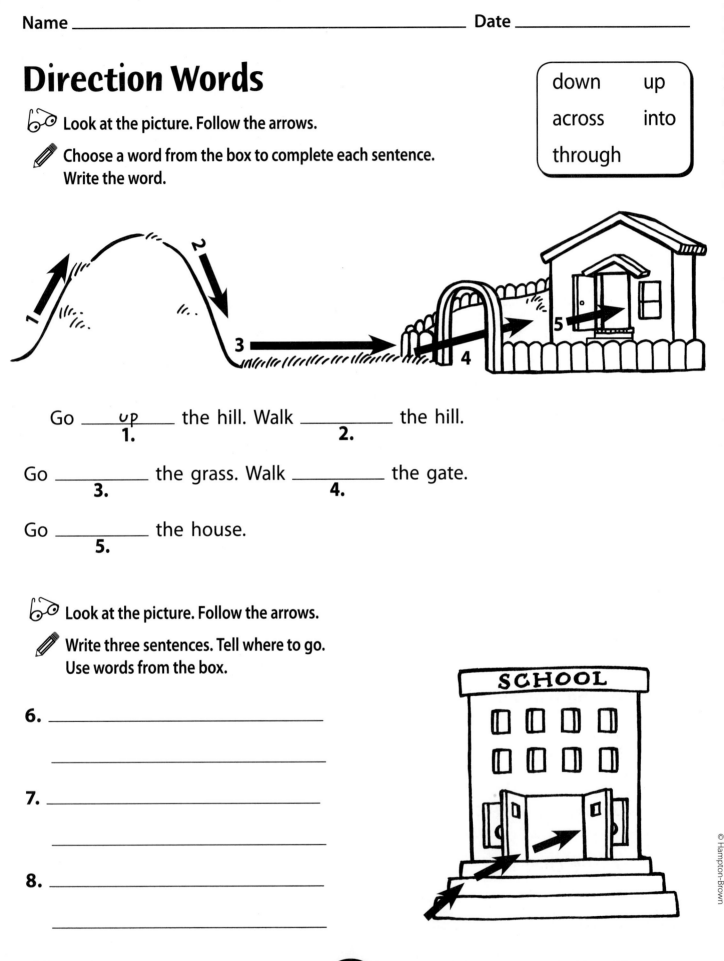

Verbs: *Was and Were*

👓 Look at pages 8–9 in *The Brother Who Gave Rice*.

✏️ Complete each sentence. Write *was* or *were*.

1. The children ___*were*___ at the table.

2. They _____ happy.

3. The baby _____ on the floor.

4. He _____ asleep.

5. The dishes _____ on the table.

6. The baskets _____ on the shelf.

7. The rice _____ hot.

8. The food _____ good.

9. It _____ a nice dinner.

10. The father said, "I _____ hungry. Now I'm full!"

11. The mother said, "We _____ all hungry!"

👓 Now look at page 32 in *The Brother Who Gave Rice*.

✏️ Write five sentences about the picture. Use *was* or *were*.

12. _____

13. _____

14. _____

15. _____

16. _____

Irregular Verbs

👓 Look at the picture. Read the sentences.

✏️ Change each sentence to tell about the past.
Use a verb from the box. Write the new sentence.

had	took
sat	gave
got	found
went	brought

Now	**In the Past**
1. Our family <u>goes</u> to the park.	Our family went to the park.
2. Mom <u>brings</u> a lot of food!	_____
3. We <u>find</u> a good table.	_____
4. We <u>sit</u> at the table.	_____
5. Dad <u>takes</u> out the food.	_____
6. I <u>get</u> the plates.	_____
7. I <u>give</u> rice to my brother.	_____
8. We all <u>have</u> a great time.	_____

More Irregular Verbs

👓 Look at the pictures.

✏️ Choose a word from the box to complete each sentence.
Write the word.

saw	felt
left	said
made	came

1.

Yesterday, Yong and I __came__ home from school.

2.

We _____ hungry.

3.

We _____ sandwiches.

4.

Then we _____ with our food.

5.

Mom _____ the mess.

6.

She _____ , "Clean this up!"

© Hampton-Brown

Actions in the Future

👓 Look at the picture.

✏️ Choose a word or words from the box to complete each sentence. Write the word or words.

will	is going to
Will	am going to
won't	are going to

1. "We _____are going to_____ hike to the lake!" said the ranger.

2. "_____ you hike with us?" Ruth asked Monika.

3. "Yes, I _____ hike with you," Monika said.

4. "I hope the hike _____ be long," Monika added. "I'm tired."

5. "Be careful! That bee _____ sting you," said the ranger.

6. "The sun is hot. I _____ wear my hat now," said Ruth.

7. "When _____ we eat lunch?" asked Monika.

8. "We _____ eat at 12:00," the ranger said.

Can, Could, and Would

👓 Look at each picture.

✏️ Complete the sentences. Write *can*, *could*, or *would*.

1. I ___can___ climb this rock.

   Be careful! You _____ fall.

2. I _____ like to eat lunch.

   We _____ eat here.

3. I _____ like to swim.

   The water _____ be cold!

Must and Should

👓 Look at the picture. Read the sign.

✏️ Write three sentences. Tell what Lorena *must* do when she hikes.

1. _____

   _____

2. _____

   _____

3. _____

   _____

👓 Look at the picture.

✏️ Write three sentences.
   Tell what Lorena *should* do when she hikes.

4. _____

   _____

5. _____

   _____

6. _____

   _____

RULES
Stay on the trail.
Pick up your trash.
Hike with another person.

Name _____ Date _____

Pronouns: Me, You, Us

👓 Look at each picture.

✏️ Write *me*, *you*, or *us* to complete the sentence.

1. I want to make a card for Dad. Will you help __me__ ?

2. Yes! We can work together. Then the card will be from _____ .

3. How can I help _____ ?

4. Please give _____ the scissors.

5. I'll give _____ the markers, too.

6. Dad will love this card from _____ !

Pronouns: *Him, Her*

👓 Read each sentence.

✏️ Change the underlined word to *him* or *her*.
Write the new sentence.

1. Yesterday, the kids had a party for <u>Mom</u>.

Yesterday, the kids had a party for her.

2. They made <u>Mom</u> a gift.

_____

3. Ivan asked <u>Marie</u> to get the gift.

_____

4. Marie handed the gift to <u>Ivan</u>.

_____

5. Ivan gave the gift to <u>Mom</u>.

_____

6. Mom smiled and hugged <u>Ivan</u>.

_____

7. Mom hugged <u>Marie</u>, too.

_____

8. Then Mom showed <u>Dad</u> the gift.

_____

Pronouns: *It, Them*

Look at pages 18–21 in *Bring Me Three Gifts!*

Read each sentence. Change the underlined words to *it* or *them*.
Write the new sentence.

1. The wives had <u>three gifts</u>.

The wives had them. _____

2. The first wife held <u>the lantern</u>.

_____

3. The second wife waved <u>the fan</u>.

_____

4. The third wife carried <u>the chimes</u>.

_____

5. Father liked <u>the gifts</u>.

_____

6. He smiled at <u>the three wives</u>.

_____

Now look at pages 24–25 in *Bring Me Three Gifts!*

Write two sentences about the picture. Use *it* and *them*.

Read your sentences to a partner. Point to the things in the picture to show *it* or *them*.

7. _____

8. _____

Name _____ Date _____

Questions with *Do* and *Does*

👓 Look at the picture. Think of questions to ask each girl.

✏️ Write your questions.

👫 Trade papers with a partner.

✏️ Answer your partner's questions.

1. Question: _Do you like to sleep outside?_____

  Answer: _Yes, I do!_____

2. Question: _Does_____

  Answer: _____

3. Question: _Do_____

  Answer: _____

4. Question: _Does_____

  Answer: _____

5. Question: _Do_____

  Answer: _____

6. Question: _Does_____

  Answer: _____

Questions with Why

✏️ Draw a line to the words that finish each question.

1. Why is   Hodja sleep outside?

2. Why does   Kemal so unhappy?

3. Why do   Hodja's eyes closed?

4. Why are   Kemal and Hodja go to Kemal's house?

📖 Look at *Does a Candle Keep You Warm?*

✏️ Write four more questions about the story or the characters.

👫 Trade papers with a partner. Answer your partner's questions.

5. Question: __Why_____

   Answer: _____

6. Question: __Why_____

   Answer: _____

7. Question: __Why_____

   Answer: _____

8. Question: __Why_____

   Answer: _____

Name _____ Date _____

Questions with How

👓 Look at the picture.

✏️ Write questions about the picture.
Use *How*, *How much*, or *How many*.

🧍🧍 Trade papers with a partner.

✏️ Answer your partner's questions.

1. Question: How strong is the wind?

 Answer: It is very strong!

2. Question: _____

 Answer: _____

3. Question: _____

 Answer: _____

4. Question: _____

 Answer: _____

5. Question: _____

 Answer: _____

6. Question: _____

 Answer: _____

Adjectives with -er and -est

✏️ Choose the correct form of the adjective to complete each sentence.
Write the word.

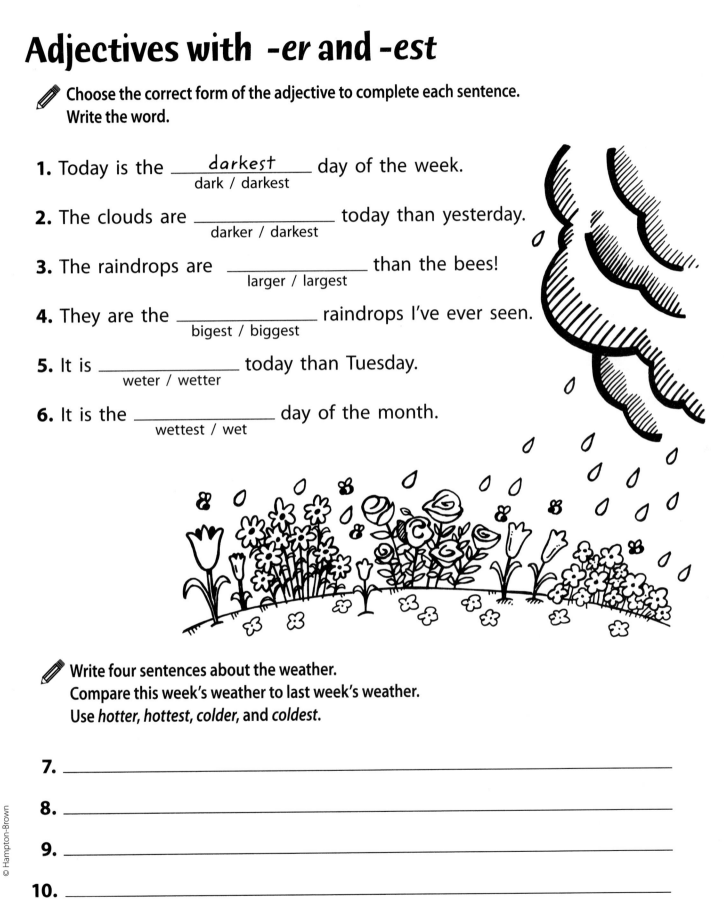

1. Today is the ____darkest____ day of the week.
   dark / darkest

2. The clouds are _____ today than yesterday.
   darker / darkest

3. The raindrops are _____ than the bees!
   larger / largest

4. They are the _____ raindrops I've ever seen.
   bigest / biggest

5. It is _____ today than Tuesday.
   weter / wetter

6. It is the _____ day of the month.
   wettest / wet

✏️ Write four sentences about the weather.
Compare this week's weather to last week's weather.
Use *hotter, hottest, colder,* and *coldest.*

7. _____

8. _____

9. _____

10. _____

Adjectives with *More* and *Most*

✏️ Complete each sentence. Use *more* or *most* with the word below the blank. Write the words.

1. Daughter Mouse is ___*more beautiful*___ than the stars.
   beautiful

2. She is the _____ mouse in the world!
   beautiful

3. Field Mouse is _____ than the Sun.
   powerful

4. He is the _____ one of all!
   powerful

5. Daughter Mouse thinks love is _____ than beauty.
   important

6. Love is the _____ thing in the universe.
   important

✏️ Draw a picture about something exciting and interesting. Write four sentences about it. Use *more* and *most*.

7. _____

8. _____

9. _____

10. _____

Name _____ Date _____

Comparisons with *Good* and *Bad*

👓 Look at the picture.

✏️ Choose the correct form of the adjective to complete each sentence. Write the word.

1. The mice have a _____*good*_____ time at the party.
good / best

2. It is the _____ party all year!
better / best

3. The cake is delicious. It is really _____ .
worse / good

4. The cake is _____ than the cookies.
better / gooder

5. Poor Papa Mouse is a _____ dancer!
worse / bad

6. He is a _____ dancer than Mama Mouse.
worse / worst

7. Papa Mouse is the _____ dancer in the family.
worst / baddest

8. He is happy, though. This is the _____ day in his life!
better / best

Writing Help

STEP ① Prewrite

Plan what you will write.

- Think of ideas.
- Choose an idea.
- Decide who your readers will be.
- Write details about your idea.

STEP ② Draft

Write fast. Turn your details into sentences. Don't worry about mistakes!

STEP ③ Revise

Make changes. Talk about your draft with a partner. Ask:

✓ Did I use good words?

✓ Is my writing interesting?

✓ Is everything in order?

✓ Did I include enough details?

Revising and Proofreading Marks

Mark	Meaning
∧	Add.
ꝰ	Take out.
ꝰ	Change to this.
⌒	Move to here.
⋏	Add a comma.
⊙	Add a period.
≡	Capitalize.
○	Check spelling.

STEP ④ Edit and Proofread

Look for mistakes. Check spelling and punctuation.

STEP ⑤ Publish

Make a final copy of your work. Share it with family and friends.

I'm a Big Fan!

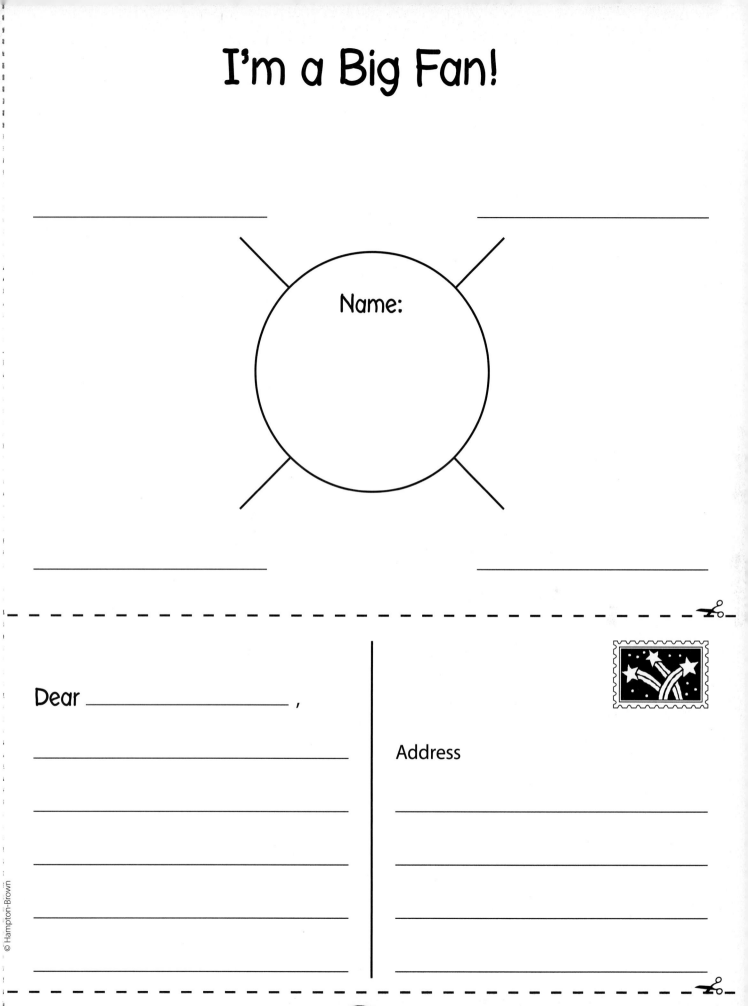

Name:

Dear _____ ,

_____

_____

_____

_____

Address

_____

_____

_____

I Am La Luna | Verbs: *Am, Is, Are*

My Picture Album

_____

_____

_____

_____

_____

_____

_____

_____

_____

_____

_____

_____

Interview

1. What is your name?

   _____

2. Where are you from?

   _____

3. When is your birthday?

   _____

4. Who is in your family? _____

   _____

5. Can you _____

   _____

6. Can you _____

   _____

7. _____

   _____

What Happens?

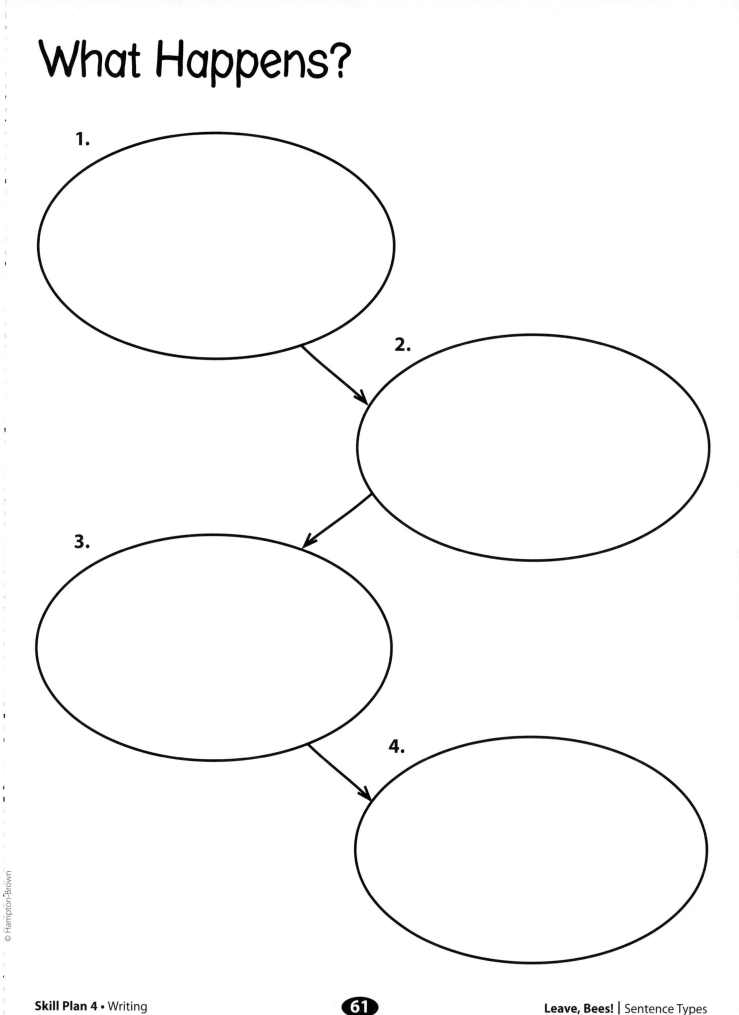

1.

2.

3.

4.

"The Elephants and the Bees" By _____

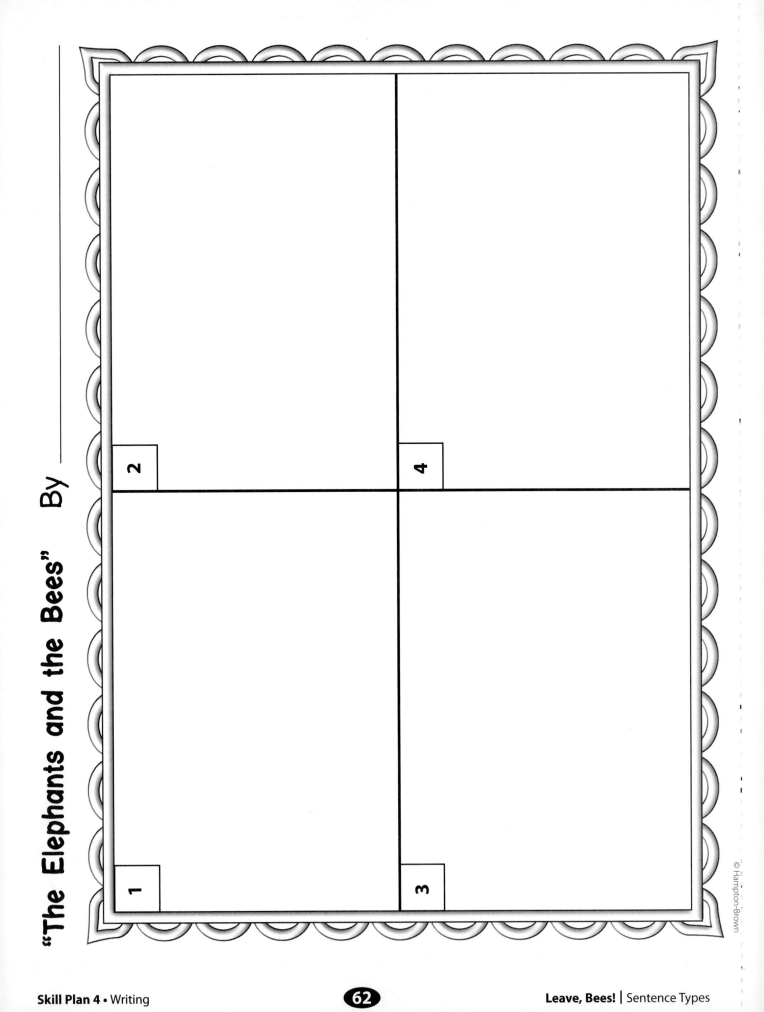

1

2

3

4

© Hampton-Brown

Survey

Time: _____ in the ❑ morning ❑ evening
                               ❑ afternoon ❑ night

What are you doing?

Activity	Number of People

What Is Everyone Doing?

Time: _____ in the

☐ morning   ☐ evening
☐ afternoon ☐ night

_____

_____

_____

_____

_____

_____

_____

_____

_____

_____

_____

_____

_____

Do You Have Pets?

1. What pets do you have?

2. How many do you have?

Name	Pets

Pets in My School

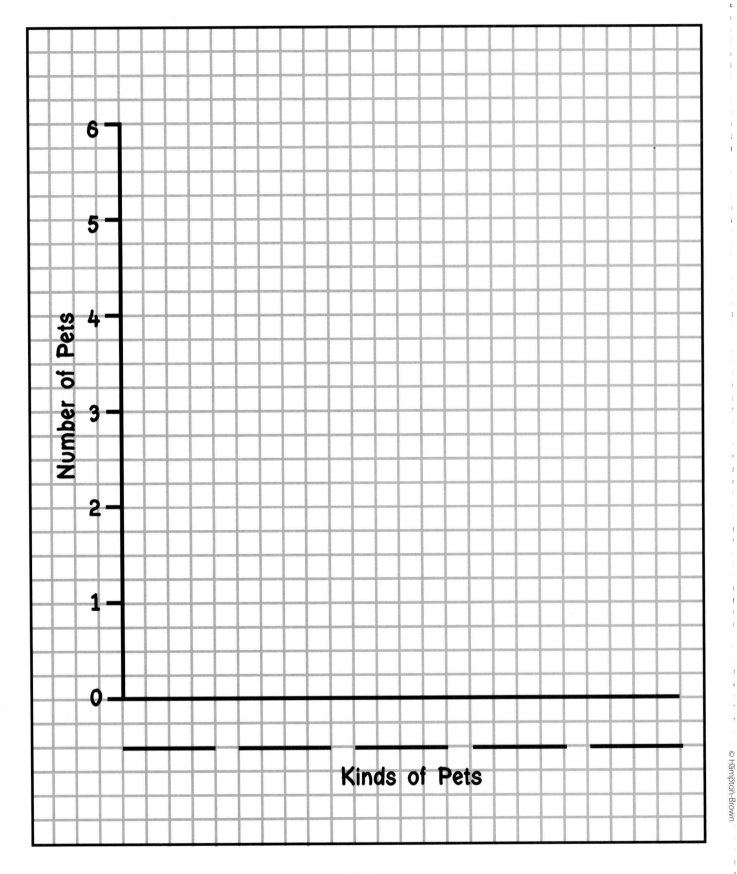

Number of Pets

6 —
5 —
4 —
3 —
2 —
1 —
0 —

Kinds of Pets

© Hampton-Brown

My Best Gift

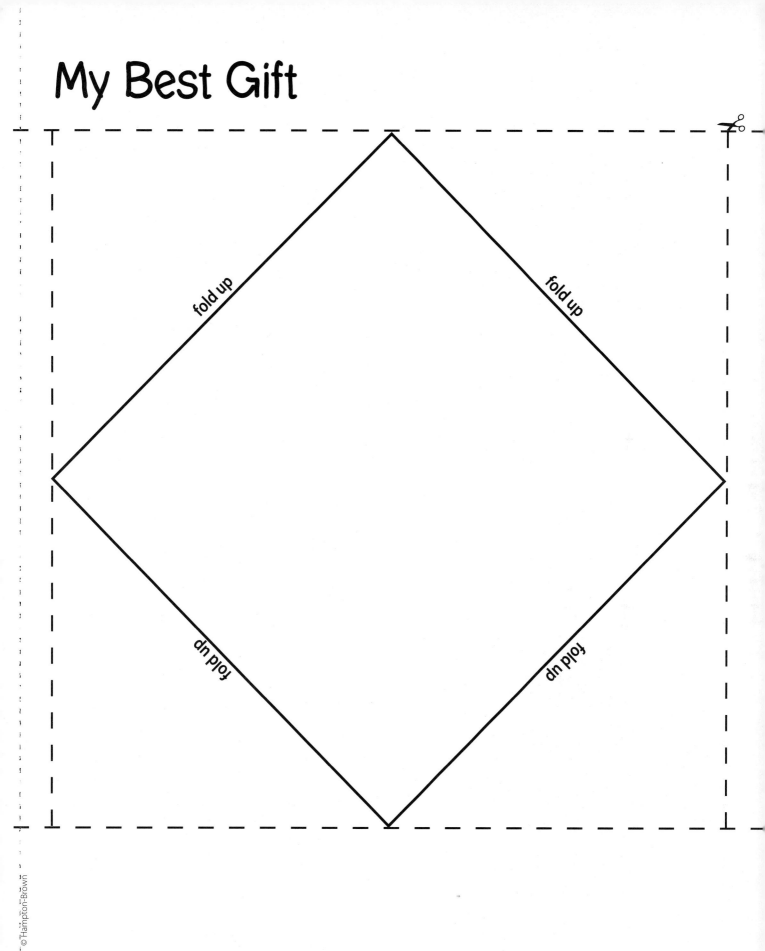

fold up

fold up

fold up

fold up

All About My Gift

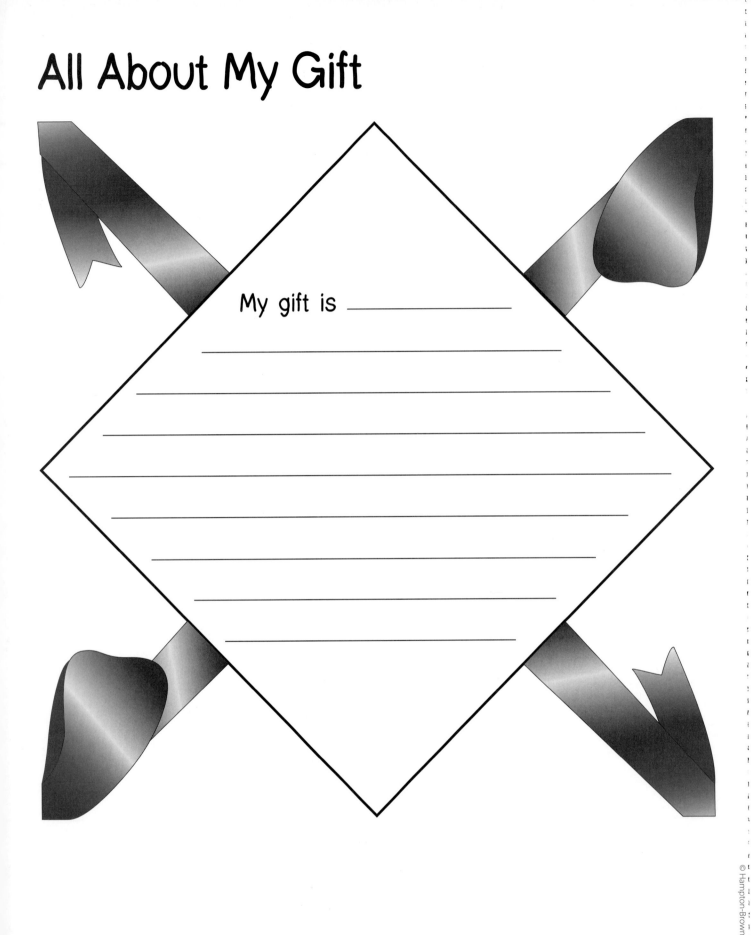

My gift is _____

_____

_____

_____

_____

_____

_____

What Happens?

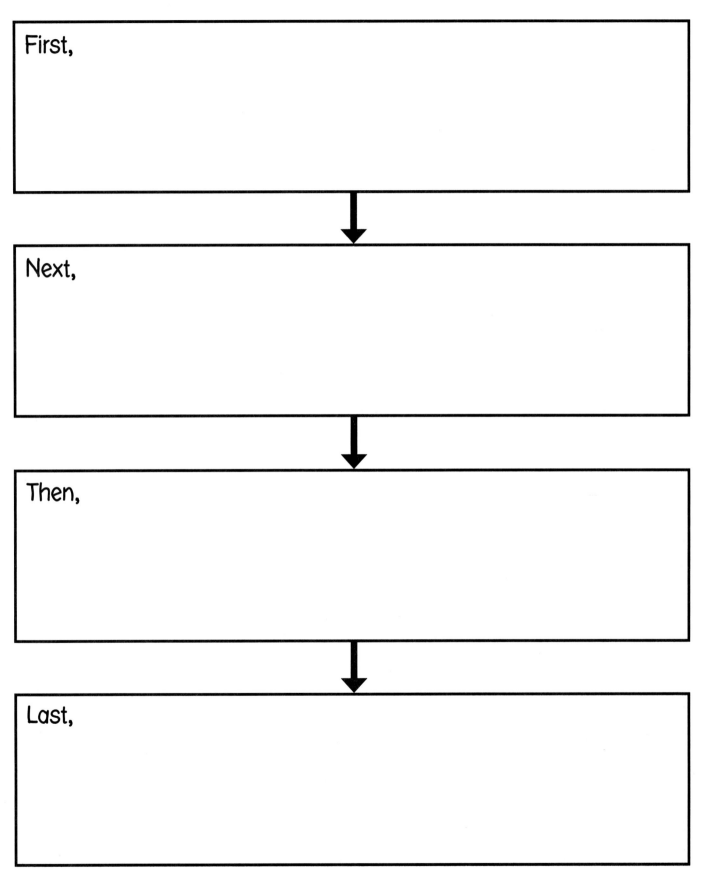

First,

Next,

Then,

Last,

© Hampton-Brown

My Sports Report

By _____

_____

_____

_____

_____

_____

_____

© Hampton-Brown

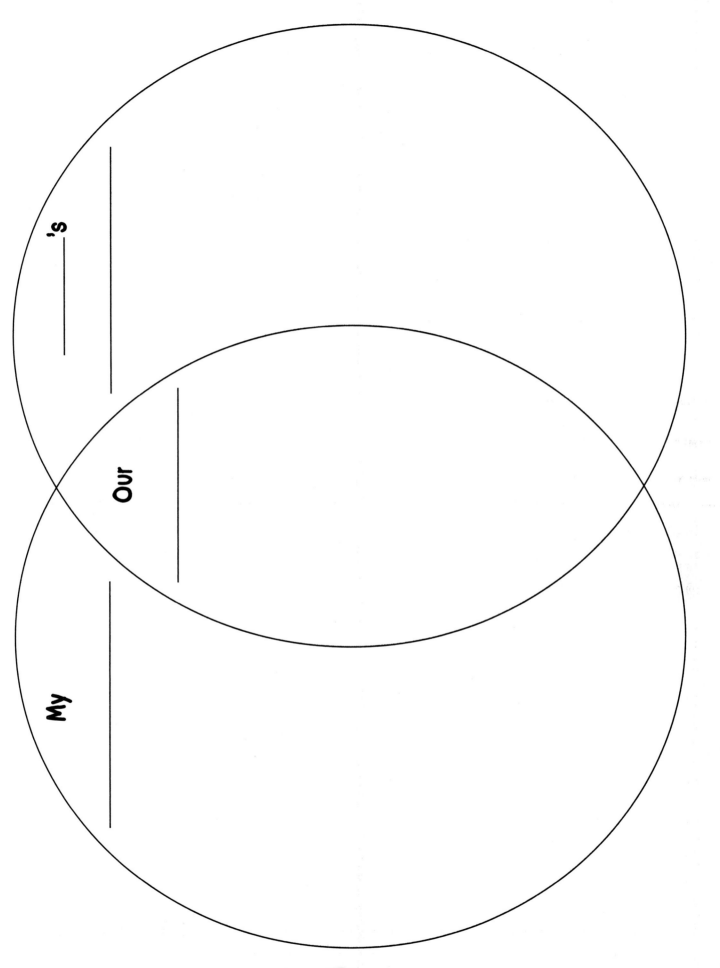

's

Our

My

© Hampton-Brown

Our _____

_____

_____

_____

_____

_____

_____

_____

_____

_____

Story Map

CHARACTERS

SETTING

PLOT

Beginning:

Middle:

End:

Title: _____

By _____

_____

_____

_____

_____

_____

_____

_____

_____

_____

_____

Main Idea: My favorite place is _____

into

under

behind

next to

in front of

on

over

across

inside

in back of

My Favorite Place

By _____

_____

_____

_____

_____

_____

_____

_____

_____

_____

_____

_____

_____

_____

A Story About Me

Main Idea:

Detail:

Detail:

Detail:

Detail:

Title: _____

By _____

_____

_____

_____

_____

_____

_____

_____

_____

Dear Know-It-All,

My problem is: _____

_____

_____

_____

_____

My question is: _____

_____

_____

Thank you,

_____

Dear _____,

_____

_____

_____

_____

_____

_____

_____

_____

_____

_____

_____

_____

Signed,

Know-It-All

What Happened

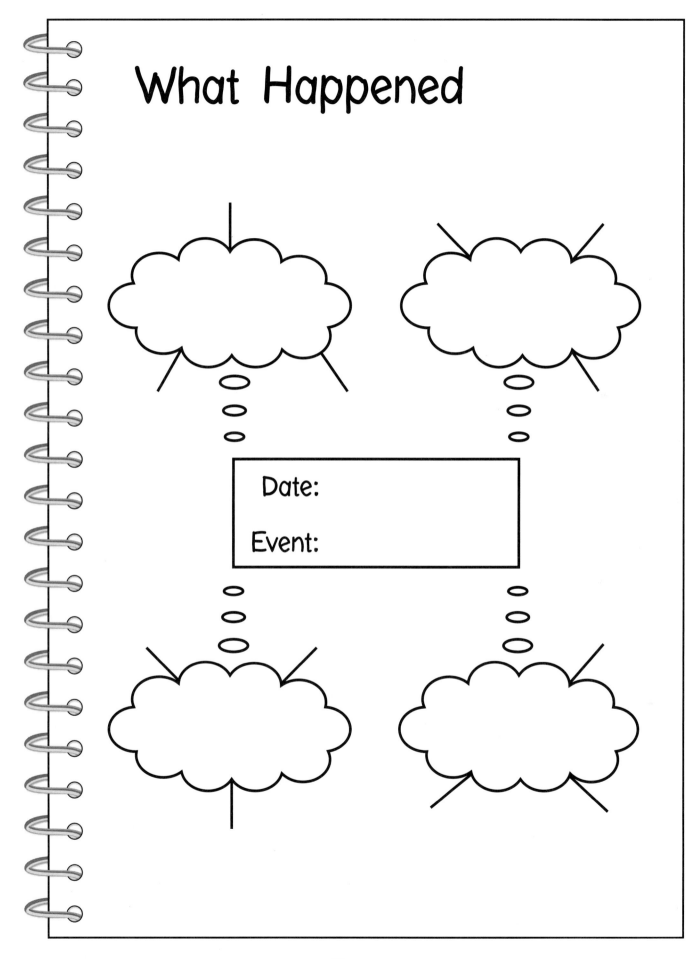

Date:

Event:

Date: _____

_____

_____

_____

_____

_____

_____

_____

_____

_____

_____

_____

_____

_____

_____

_____

_____

_____

_____

Our Script Planner

Questions	Answers
_____ asks:	_____ answers:
_____ asks:	_____ answers:
_____ asks:	_____ answers:
_____ asks:	_____ answers:

Our Script

Character	Dialogue
_____	_____
_____	_____
_____	_____
_____	_____
_____	_____
_____	_____
_____	_____

My Review of:

Title: _____

By: _____

Illustrated by: _____

This book is _____ than other books. It is _____

_____

_____

_____

_____

You
☐ should
☐ should not   read this book!

Good things about this book:

Bad things about this book:

This book is about _____

Skill Tests

Skill Test 1

DIRECTIONS Look at each picture. What word or words are missing?
Mark your answer.

1. Ⓐ is
   Ⓑ am
   Ⓒ are
   Ⓓ I'm

2. Ⓕ I
   Ⓖ am
   Ⓗ You
   Ⓙ You're

3. Ⓐ is
   Ⓑ am
   Ⓒ are
   Ⓓ I'm

4. Ⓕ The boots is
   Ⓖ The boot are
   Ⓗ The boots am
   Ⓙ The boots are

Skill Test 2

DIRECTIONS Look at each picture. What word is missing?
Mark your answer.

1. (A) I
    (B) He
    (C) We
    (D) You

2. (F) I
    (G) It
    (H) He
    (J) She

3. (A) It
    (B) We
    (C) She
    (D) They

4. (F) It
    (G) You
    (H) She
    (J) They

Skill Test 3

DIRECTIONS Look at each picture. What word or words are missing?
Mark your answer.

1. Ⓐ I can
   Ⓑ I, yes
   Ⓒ Can you
   Ⓓ Yes, you

2. Ⓕ Soup is it
   Ⓖ Soup it are
   Ⓗ Is the soup
   Ⓙ Are the soup

3. Ⓐ Is the ball
   Ⓑ The ball is
   Ⓒ Where ball is
   Ⓓ The ball where

4. Ⓕ Who
   Ⓖ What
   Ⓗ When
   Ⓙ Where

Skill Test 4

DIRECTIONS Look at each picture. What words are missing?
Mark your answer.

1.
Ⓐ Is this
Ⓑ Can you
Ⓒ Open you
Ⓓ Please open

2.
Ⓕ Can I
Ⓖ I have
Ⓗ Have I
Ⓙ What is

3.
Ⓐ Is not
Ⓑ See you
Ⓒ Where is
Ⓓ Is where

4.
Ⓕ not quiet are
Ⓖ are quiet not
Ⓗ not are quiet
Ⓙ are not quiet

Skill Test 5

DIRECTIONS Look at each picture. What words are missing?
Mark your answer.

1. Ⓐ is eats
   Ⓑ are eat
   Ⓒ is eating
   Ⓓ are eating

2. Ⓕ is plays
   Ⓖ are play
   Ⓗ is playing
   Ⓙ are playing

3. Ⓐ Is he
   Ⓑ Am he
   Ⓒ He are
   Ⓓ Are he

4. Ⓕ buying not am
   Ⓖ not am buying
   Ⓗ buying am not
   Ⓙ am not buying

Skill Test 6

DIRECTIONS Look at each picture. What word or words are missing?
Mark your answer.

1. Ⓐ a ducks
   Ⓑ an ducks
   Ⓒ three duck
   Ⓓ three ducks

2. Ⓕ a orange
   Ⓖ an orange
   Ⓗ two orange
   Ⓙ two oranges

3. Ⓐ mice
   Ⓑ mices
   Ⓒ mouse
   Ⓓ mouses

4. Ⓕ child
   Ⓖ childs
   Ⓗ children
   Ⓙ childrens

Skill Test 7

DIRECTIONS Look at each picture. What word or words are missing?
Mark your answer.

1. Ⓐ that
   Ⓑ two
   Ⓒ three
   Ⓓ square

2. Ⓕ big gift
   Ⓖ gift big
   Ⓗ little gift
   Ⓙ gift little

3. Ⓐ grape is sweet
   Ⓑ are grapes sweet
   Ⓒ sweet grapes are
   Ⓓ grapes are sweet

4. Ⓕ This
   Ⓖ That
   Ⓗ These
   Ⓙ Those

Name _____ Date _____

Skill Test 8

DIRECTIONS Look at each picture. What words are missing?
Mark your answer.

1. (A) I jump
    (B) I jumps
    (C) They jump
    (D) They jumps

2. (F) Play we
    (G) We play
    (H) We plays
    (J) Playing we

3. (A) Monica climb
    (B) Monica climbs
    (C) Climbs Monica
    (D) Monica climbing

4. (F) She has
    (G) Has she
    (H) She have
    (J) She haves

Skill Test 9

DIRECTIONS Look at each picture. What word is missing?
Mark your answer.

1. Ⓐ Dad
    Ⓑ Dads
    Ⓒ Dads'
    Ⓓ Dad's

2. Ⓕ I
    Ⓖ my
    Ⓗ his
    Ⓙ their

3. Ⓐ Its
    Ⓑ His
    Ⓒ Her
    Ⓓ Their

4. Ⓕ it
    Ⓖ its
    Ⓗ they
    Ⓙ their

Skill Test 10

DIRECTIONS Look at each picture. What word is missing?
Mark your answer.

1. Ⓐ like
　 Ⓑ likd
　 Ⓒ likes
　 Ⓓ liking

2. Ⓕ land
　 Ⓖ laned
　 Ⓗ landed
　 Ⓙ landing

3. Ⓐ jump
　 Ⓑ jumped
　 Ⓒ jumping
　 Ⓓ jumpped

4. Ⓕ hops
　 Ⓖ hoped
　 Ⓗ hopped
　 Ⓙ hopping

Skill Test 11

DIRECTIONS Look at each picture. What word is missing?
Mark your answer.

1. Ⓐ in
   Ⓑ on
   Ⓒ below
   Ⓓ behind

2. Ⓕ on
   Ⓖ beside
   Ⓗ behind
   Ⓙ between

3. Ⓐ in
   Ⓑ on
   Ⓒ over
   Ⓓ under

4. Ⓕ up
   Ⓖ into
   Ⓗ down
   Ⓙ through

Skill Test 12

DIRECTIONS Look at each picture. What word is missing?
Mark your answer.

1. Ⓐ are
    Ⓑ had
    Ⓒ was
    Ⓓ were

2. Ⓕ take
    Ⓖ took
    Ⓗ taked
    Ⓙ tooked

3. Ⓐ has
    Ⓑ had
    Ⓒ have
    Ⓓ haved

4. Ⓕ ate
    Ⓖ eat
    Ⓗ ated
    Ⓙ eated

Skill Test 13

DIRECTIONS Look at each picture. What word or words are missing?
Mark your answer.

1. Ⓐ am
Ⓑ are
Ⓒ will
Ⓓ going

2. Ⓕ is going to
Ⓖ am going to
Ⓗ will going to
Ⓙ can going to

3. Ⓐ must
Ⓑ going
Ⓒ could
Ⓓ should

4. Ⓕ are
Ⓖ must
Ⓗ going
Ⓙ would

© Hampton-Brown

Name _____ Date _____

Skill Test 14

DIRECTIONS Look at each picture. What word is missing?
Mark your answer.

1. Ⓐ it
Ⓑ me
Ⓒ you
Ⓓ them

2. Ⓕ me
Ⓖ we
Ⓗ you
Ⓙ him

3. Ⓐ me
Ⓑ her
Ⓒ him
Ⓓ them

4. Ⓕ it
Ⓖ us
Ⓗ him
Ⓙ them

Skill Test 15

DIRECTIONS Look at each picture. What words are missing?
Mark your answer.

1.
- Ⓐ I do
- Ⓑ Do you
- Ⓒ You does
- Ⓓ Does you

2.
- Ⓕ The bug do
- Ⓖ Do the bug
- Ⓗ Bug the does
- Ⓙ Does the bug

3.
- Ⓐ Do are they
- Ⓑ Are why they
- Ⓒ Why are they
- Ⓓ Why how they

4.
- Ⓕ How is
- Ⓖ How are
- Ⓗ How many
- Ⓙ How much

Name _____   Date _____

Skill Test 16

DIRECTIONS Look at each picture. What word or words are missing?
Mark your answer.

1. ⒶＡ nice
Ⓑ nicer
Ⓒ niceer
Ⓓ nicest

2. Ⓕ the hotter day
Ⓖ hotter day than
Ⓗ hottest the day
Ⓙ the hottest day

3. Ⓐ more exciting
Ⓑ most exciting
Ⓒ more excitinger
Ⓓ most excitingest

4. Ⓕ best
Ⓖ better
Ⓗ bestest
Ⓙ goodest

ACKNOWLEDGMENTS

Illustrations

Karen Stormer Brooks: p12 (kite), p36, pp40-44, p46, p48, p89, pp91-103; **Joe Cepeda:** p19; **Eva Vagreti Cockrille:** p15; **Lynne Cravath:** p3, p4, pp6-11, p13, pp16-18, pp20-21, p22 (boy), pp25-26, p29, p32, p35, pp37-39, p88, p90; **Ruth Flanigan:** p22 (birthday illustrations), p23; **Peter Grosshauser:** pp49-51; **Jennifer Hewitson:** p27; **Maurie Manning:** p34; **Deborah Melmon:** p14, p31, p33; **Cheryl Kirk Noll:** p5, p24, p45, p47; **Ana Ochoa:** p28, p30; **Wendy Rasmussen:** p12 (lunch, swing, bread), p59.

Hampton-Brown
P.O. Box 223220
Carmel, California 93922
800-333-3510
www.hampton-brown.com

Printed in the United States of America

ISBN 0-7362-2498-X

07 08 09 10 11 12 13 14 10 9 8 7 6 5 4